Sancti Clandestini
Undercover Saints

Maggie Butt

Ward Wood Publishing
www.wardwoodpublishing.co.uk

Published by Ward Wood Publishing
6 The Drive
Golders Green
London NW11 9SR
www.wardwoodpublishing.co.uk

The right of Maggie Butt to be identified as author of the poetry has been asserted by her in accordance with the Copyright, Designs and Patent Act, 1988.
Copyright © 2012 Maggie Butt

Copyright of individual illustrations remains with each illustrator.
The moral right of illustrators has been asserted.
Full details of copyright holders can be found on page 74.

ISBN 978-1-908742-13-1

British Library Cataloguing in Publication Data. A CIP record for this book can be obtained from the British Library.

Designed and typeset in Palatino Linotype
by Nancy Slonims and Laura Alvarado

Cover Design by Nancy Slonims and Laura Alvarado
Cover Artwork: Kateryna Boiko

Printed and bound in Great Britain by
Imprint Digital, Seychelles Farm,
Upton Pyne, Exeter EX5 5HY.

Dedication

To the generous and gifted staff and students
of Middlesex University's BA Illustration course.

Acknowledgements

These poems (or versions of them) have appeared in
*Acumen, The Bow Wow Shop, The London Magazine,
Orbis, Envoi, Equinox, The French Literary Review,
petite (Hearing Eye), Snap (Templar).*

Thanks to Cheryl Moskovitz and Helena Nelson for
close reading, and the suggestion to team the poems
with illustrations. Thanks to Helena Blakemore for
her unquenchable enthusiam. Thanks to my friends
in the North London Stanza group and to June Hall
for support and advice. Special thanks to Martin Ursell
for his work with the illustrators, and to Nancy Slonims,
the fairy godmother who turned a wish into a book.

Contents:

There are official Patron Saints of wax-melters, truss makers, lumberjacks, Florentine cheese merchants and disappointing children.

This book proposes some alternative, imaginary saints.

The Patron Saints of:

Remaindered Books	13
Careless Cyclists	14
Missed Connections	17
Liars	19
Compulsive Hoarders	20
Infidel Girls	23
The Un-Cool	24
Undelivered Letters	26
Naps	29
Rank Outsiders	31
Obsessive Housewives	33
Sunday Morning	35
Poetic Words	36
Weekends	39
English Country Dancing	41
Sat Navs	42
Tattoos	44
Old Dogs	47
Enthusiasts	48
Eco-Warriors	51
Bullies	52
Looters	55
Soda Giants	56
Hoods	59
Haunted Houses	60
Unwanted Hope	63
The End of the World	65
Whistling	66
Conferences	69
Ugly Towns	70
Poets	73

Sancti Clandestini

Undercover Saints

The Patron Saint of Remaindered Books

She haunts the bargain bookshops,
calls them to her softly, hears the faint
flutterings among their leaves,
as stray cats would purr and rub
themselves against her shins;

she gathers them, abandoned children
living on scraps in a shanty town,
fighting seagulls on the rubbish heap,
ekeing out echoes of their rave reviews,
envying the few, scornful of best-sellers;

she garners them – a harvest-home
where every one is dusted, shelved
in the eternal Dewey Decimal.

The Patron Saint of Careless Cyclists

I glimpsed her once
(in Holland naturally)
as their bike flashed
along the cycle track,
her neat bum balanced
on her lover's handlebars,
back to the future,
legs around his waist,
kissing with blind passion
steered by love.

The Patron Saint of Missed Connections

She mourns: the nine-fifteen which failed to spill
its passengers in time to wing their flight;

the eyes which meet across the bar but neither
moves or speaks, although they thought they might;

the phone which burrs and purrs with urgent love
for one who never knows he tried to call;

the girl who checks *Arrivals* all in vain
and hopes, until the cleaner sweeps the hall;

those on the line where ancient steam-wreathed trains
chug through the stations, where they never stop.

She tries to bring them running through the rain
into the chance-meet table-clothed tea shop.

The Patron Saint of Liars

She is adroit with all the daisy-like
simplicities: *Your hair looks nice,*
I like your dress, What a bonny babe.

She is beatific as she strews the petals
of *You're looking well, How clever!*
It's no trouble and *My pleasure.*

But canonise her for the scented
bouquets of *It doesn't hurt, I slept quite*
well and *Everything will be all right.*

The Patron Saint of Compulsive Hoarders

She's grown to one of those old girls
who squirrel everything away, who wrap

each empty sardine tin in newsprint,
build them tenderly like dry stone walls,

who wash out jam jars, pile them
to the ceiling, glinting in their pent-up

usefulness. She stores discarded children's
board games, milk-teeth, crusts, soft toys

(gathering a faint grey of dust, an extra
fluff of plush), in case time should swing

open like a door and find her lost in past
without that very thing she loved the most;

to raise defences against any loss,
to guard against that sharp twist of regret,

or helter-skelter to a future where it is
the very thing she needs to save the human race.

The Patron Saints of Infidel Girls

They watch her from behind black burqas.
She climbs aboard the bus, drags
ruck-sack, sweat darkening her T shirt.

As the bus grinds along the desert road
four of them rise from their separate seats,
advance towards her down the bone-shake aisle.

Despite herself, she thinks of crows
winging in to feast on carrion;
shifts in her seat, crosses suntanned arms.

They settle themselves around her,
naked in their eyes, without hijab,
language-less and just a girl (my girl)

pink and defenceless as a baby;
four silent, black-clad guardian angels
at her head and hands and feet.

The Patron Saint of the Un-Cool

She stands at play-time by each skinny,
speccy, breathy, spotty kid, absorbs
the taunts of bullies, smelts them into
white hot anger and ambition.

She leans into the minds of the ultra
cool, fills their brains with hair-styles,
make-up, cars and football, who said what;
puts out a foot and trips them in exams.

She dresses teenage geeks in ballet skirts
and hobnail boots, dyes hair blue-black,
celebrates strangeness, sets them outside
where they get the clearest view.

She grows them up to be the physicists,
the software millionaires, the novelists;
the ones who have the last laugh
grinning over their Nobel prizes.

APPLIED CHEMISTRY FOR GIRLS

RVEY F. EHLER

LAKEWOOD PRINTING CO.

THE ROMANCE OF STAMP COLLECTING

ERNEST A. KEHR

THOMAS CROWELL

POETRY FOR THE YOUNG * CHIZO A. ANIMALU

UCHEAKONAM FOUNDATION

SO YOU WANT TO BE A LIBRARIAN

Lauren Pressley

Library Jiuce Press

THE BOYS' AND GIRLS' BOOK OF SCIENCE

NABU PRESS

THE YOUNG ACCOUNTANT'S SHEET: OR DOUBLE ENTRY AT A GLANCE

WILLIAM GILL

WILLIAM DINZEY BURTON

THE YOUNG BEEKEEPER

HARRY MGNIGOL

WARNE

THE BOYS' BOOK OF RAILWAYS

J.R. HOWDEN

FREDERICK A. STOKES

The Patron Saint of Undelivered Letters

Feel her warm breath beside your ear,
her fingers wrapped around your own,
her eyes which follow pen or screen;
each word you know you should, each
word you wish you could; the ones
you write and never post. She tips
your hesitating hand into the pillar box,
or else she whispers *Wait* before you
angrily hit *Send*. She rights a million
wrongs in recompense for that slim
note which Tess once slipped beneath
his door and underneath the rug.

The Patron Saint of Naps

She'll send you where the poker players go,
the night owls, bar maids, croupiers,
call girls, DJs, doctors, nurses,
all night newsmen, anxious students.

She loves the sigh of bed springs over Spain,
Flamenco dancers kicking off their shoes,
the gentle snores of dreaming matadors
sleeping off Rioja drunk at noon.

She shows you tabbies, Persians, mogs,
seeking out a sunny patch to curl;
nothing more delicious than to nap
in daylight, while the others toil.

The Patron Saint of Rank Outsiders

The old men in the betting shop
have heard him cough and spit
and felt his fingers on their shoulders:

Remember Cassius and Sonny,
Sunderland and Leeds, Foinavon,
a hundred to one. Go on, try.

And so, improbably, a tumour
vanishes from someone's gut;
a man falls from an aeroplane

through thunderclouds and storms,
and lives; a pretty girl will love
a man with neither wealth or looks;

a child will surface, breathing,
after twenty minutes in the freezing
waves; it will rain frogs in Hertfordshire.

The Patron Saint of Obsessive Housewives

She loves the ones who make their husbands
walk on newspaper around the house, who wake

to see, with horror, a small discolouration
on the bedroom ceiling, are up at dawn

each day to scrub and rinse and polish.
She tells them nothing's ever clean or bright

enough, no product kills that last % of germs,
she know the hours of the day too short to fight

the fiend of dirt. Without her help the world's
too grimy, its flood-waters lap their sewage

round the island of the house, threaten
to spill its filth into their lives. Infections

buzz at every window pane, on every
shoe, its muck, so close, so close.

The Patron Saint of Sunday Morning

A sky of milk and grey-pearl
droops to the streets, close
enough to touch; fine mizzle nets
my hair, damps cheeks and clothes.

Lost clouds drift through the streets:
one smudged-make-up girl shivers
in her red frock and high heels, walks
the walk of shame; a woman

lights a candle in the cathedral, slow
over the flame; a man hunches in pain.
Each dressed in a patina of drizzle,
tenuous as ghosts. I step round the droppings

of the night-fox, the vomit of revellers,
almost walk into the saint herself,
the dumpy Indian woman in a track-suit,
who wishes me *Good Morning*, unlocks

a future full of possibility, words falling
like a promise, a blessing on the day.

The Patron Saint of Poetic Words

He sidles close and slips
them like a drug into my drink,
they scatter from my pen as freely
as 'f' words in a playground.

See them fly like pigeons from a loft:
luminous, iridescent, shimmering,
myriad, miasma, moonlit,
beauteous, wondrous, joyous.

I turn my back on him and cross them out:
~~*myriad, miasma, moonlit*~~.
But ah! sometimes the world is
luminous, iridescent, shimmering.

The Patron Saint of Weekends

He has a way of teasing out the hours
like combs through tangled locks; unfurls
the daylight, slower than a frond of fern.

He orchestrates the afternoon: the bass-line
blur of cars in never ending busyness;
the twitter of small birds announcing

greenfly feasts; a distant peal of bells
to celebrate a wedding; the swell
of guitar over PA from a summer fete;

bursts of Greensleeves from the ice-cream
van as it meanders up and down the streets
of Sunday afternoons long gone.

The Patron Saint of English Country Dancing

The frost comes down as hard as grief,
mums queue for food which can't be found,
whole streets leave comfy beds each night,
sleep sardined, airless, underground.
Do-si-do, cross hands, straight hay,
Fall back, cast off, cast round,
And gallop up the set…

Young teacher with her London kids,
head full of tunes and English soul,
marooned on a mountainside in Wales
with schoolroom boiler out of coal.
Do-si-do, cross hands, straight hay,
Fall back, cast off, cast round,
And gallop up the set…

She sends the big boys out for wood
and piles the desks against the wall,
to thaw the rest with country dance
she'll play and sing and clap and call:
Do-si-do, cross hands, straight hay,
Fall back, cast off, cast round,
And gallop up the set…

Weave *Shrewsbury Lasses, Buttered Pease,*
transported to a pre-war dream;
Sir Roger de Coverley leads
them home, *All In A Garden Green*.

The Patron Saint of Sat Navs

I answer centuries of prayer,
for you were lost, but failed to specify
the time-frame to be found.

I watch you from above, like saints of old
and guide you with my kindly hints,
Turn around where possible.

The downside is that now you're truly lost,
your hand in mine as trusting as a child
with no idea of where you've been or go.

I am two hours away you faithfully repeat,
because I told you so. Medieval
in belief, channeling all long-lost faith

in me. Absorb my mantras, leave
all questioning and reason in the past,
folded with maps and sextant and stars.

The Patron Saint of Tattoos

I choose the ripples of your living flesh –
my paintings breathe, sweat, shimmer, soak the sun,
not trapped in gloomy halls, or fixed on plaster
in the cold apse of a church. Oh yes, they'd last,
but not know anything of love: that certainty
of names within a heart; the scar which shows
where love once was (the name erased, though memory
still breathes); the only choice when boys go off to war
(no call for death's heads, anchors, lips and roses then).
He creeps in, sheepish, says the one word, *Mum.*
I give him that. From skin to skin he takes her
to his grave, as she goes down with him.

The Patron Saint of Old Dogs

They should be allowed to lie in the sun
twitching in rabbit-chasing dreams,
to take sedate walks, barking at squirrels,
to scoff their meaty chunks too fast,
to grow a little stout and slow, to howl
sometimes at the lonely moon.

Instead they sit up and beg my help
with new tricks: fresh ways to fetch
the mail, retrieve the files, roll over
for new masters, play dead (or harder
at times, play living), shake paws
with a future which careens towards
them like huskies pulling a sled,
balance balls on their noses, balance
the books, dance on their hind legs
and bark along to the music of time.

The Patron Saint of Enthusiasts

Glory be to God for geeky folk
who choose to ride one life-long hobby-horse.

Without them: bells hang dumb in steeples
sad breezes cannot sing their lolling tongues

footpaths revert to bramble patches, overgrown
and lost as Sleeping Beauty's castle

wounded hedgehogs bleed into the verge
and no-one counts the sparrows' fall

civil war battles are not re-enacted
so history's just words upon a page

breeding pairs of eagles are not spotted
and small boys steal their priceless eggs

bells and sticks and hankies don't cavort
all culture is homogenised TV

branch railway lines forget
the chug and puff of slower life.

A glorious fairground blares and beckons
but they spend all life's pennies at one stall –

my task to keep them focused, blinkered
so the world will be indebted to them all.

The Patron Saint of Eco-Warriors

She watches those who fiddle while earth burns,
wonders why they do not lie awake
confronting the enormity, but hope
some scientists will clever them out
of trouble, paddle their raft to safety.

She looks around for samurai
and, once she touches them, they burn
like convent girls, ablaze to truth
revealed to just the chosen few, zealous
as converts, as if their fingers
have been jammed into electric
sockets, and purpose blazes in their heads.

Thus branded, they go forth to save
the tiger, turn algae into fuel, build cars
to run on water, sail rainbow ships,
lie in front of bulldozers, wave
goodbye to families to live in tents
or trees, driven, pure as waterfalls.

She scorns the saintly micro-miracles:
stigmata, healing, water into wine.
Her sights are high; if she can pull it off
her warriors will clinch the miracle
to end all miracles – for they will save the earth.

The Patron Saint of Bullies

Bullies always prosper
that's my golden rule.
See it in the workplace,
see it in the school.

Teach your children wisely:
Nobody will tell,
let them throw their weight about
let them shout and yell.

Keep them off the naughty stair
reward them if they bite,
chairs of boards, director's posts
can be within their sights.

Teach them not to listen
or negotiate,
they will climb the ladder,
rungs of cold-steel hate.

Let him beat his sister,
it's practice for his wife.
Techniques learned in childhood
will serve him all his life.

THE PATRON SAINT OF LOOTERS

54

The Patron Saint of Looters

My acolytes, like boy scouts or wise virgins,
are always ready for the call. Their Blackberries
ping, their Facebook flickers, Twitter
tweets. The news spreads faster than jungle
drums or smoke and gives precise directions
to the glittering goal: here for TVs, there for trainers,
upgrade your mobile phones en-route.

That was our night, when law hung back
shy as an 11-year-old at a school dance,
when we made bonfires out of cars, to serve
them right for shiny smugness, kicked in
shop windows full of stuff we can't afford,
the objects advertisers dangle just beyond
our reach, to tantelise and taunt us.

The Patron Saint of Soda Giants

I love my two sons equally,
my Tweedledum and Tweedledee
engaged in battle royal. And while
they fight I make it possible
for ad campaigns to reach the darkest
heart of darkest continents
so every village chants their names,
replacing older gods.

I steer deliveries, rattling
around mine-fields, help lorries
reach the lands where UN aid
can never reach, waved through
by child militia, rifles slung
across their backs, who claim
a warm but fizzy tax, *Lipsmackin-*
thirstquenchinacetastin…

My warring sons, astride the globe,
can place a curvy bottle in the hand
of toddlers who will not live to drink
disease-free water. Rejoice! For they
will die with the Real Thing on their lips!

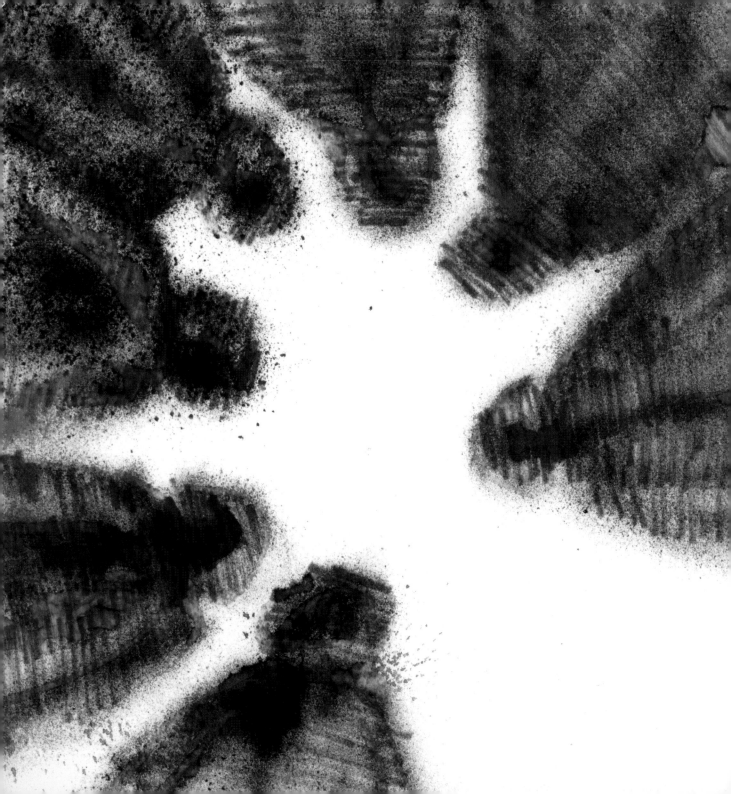

The Patron Saint of Hoods

I've played a waiting game, through centuries
of hats; survived on the odd cloak or duffel coat,

but since surveillance cameras erupted
like a syphilitic rash on every street

my medieval cunning fools technology
with a hey nonny, ho nonny, o hoodie o!

I will protect identities of gangs rampaging
through a city centre, the faces of drunks

a-vomiting, thugs a-mugging, youths
a-jeering. But how I long once more

to make invisible one who steals from the rich
at arrow-point, to give to the poor.

The Patron Saint of Haunted Houses

He wanders through hallways as dismal as dawn,
the friend of the lonely, bereft and forlorn,
he whispers in voices of those who have gone;
his charges are those who refuse to move on.

The creak of a shutter, the close of a door,
the rustle of silk or of leaves on the floor,
his breath is the palpable chill in the air,
his footfall the tap of her heels on the stair.

He'll make sure you know from the hour you arrive:
the sense of a presence no longer alive,
a dankness, the mouldering smell of a ghost,
a just-left-the-room most ungenial host.

A knock on the window, a shade in the glass
attorney to spectres, reluctant to pass,
caressing the hair to stand up on your nape
he represents those who are seeking escape,

entrapped by their misery, spirits who yearn,
their unfinished business his daily concern.
He soothes them to hush, supernaturally still,
they watch you arrive, unsuspecting, until...

Cobbett's Brake

Longmains

Clifford House

Eel-Marsh House

Chrighton Abbey

Bly

Westfield Hall

Ladlow Hall

Church Peveril

The Patron Saint of Unwanted Hope

And there he goes again
popping up, all apple-cheeks
and marmalade smiles
like a jack-in-the-box –

persistent as the couple
who overstay the party,
like an iPhone bore
longing to share his apps,

a stalker who finds your
new address and turns up
with a bottle of cheap wine
expecting a meal on the table.

Too stupid to know he's
beaten, buried, six-feet-under,
up he hops, grinning,
shaking off the clods of earth.

Just as you were moving on
finding another route
reassembling the broken
pieces of your life, he's there

scrubbed as a schoolboy,
innocent as snow, certain
there will one day be an
answer, reconciliation, cure.

The Patron Saint of The End of The World

You should see her Operations Centre:
giant plasma screens and maps and charts
more complex than a military campaign.

Think global Olympic opening ceremonies,
world-wide synchronised fire and brimstone,
seven plagues, seven stars, seven trumpets.

She waits to begin, her hair ablaze,
feet of brass, and voice like Niagara,
egging on tyrants, drumming her fingers.

Plans for the sorting yards demand
daily expansion of deserts, Sahara
and Siberia set aside for non-believers.

Every now and then she runs a drill,
sends out electric whispers that the end
is nigh, crashing down like a comet.

She monitors response: hand-painted
lettering on sandwich boards;
old prophecies unearthed, interpreted

(Nostradamus, Mayan calendar);
derision and indifference. She stamps
back to the drawing board, increases

the size of the holding pens for hell,
nudges each of us with our own taster:
the death of a dog, a friend, a child.

The Patron Saint of Whistling

He sups his pint in smoke-black corners,
with saints of thatching, tatting, flint knapping,
who all remember milkmen and delivery boys
fluting in the echoey grey of urban dawns.

For his was once the only music on the move,
the personal stereo system of the masses,
that orchestra inside your head transposed
for lips and cheeks, for trills and blows.

It was a way to feign a swaggering bravery,
to summon conscience – or more corporeal help,
a way to seem much less alone,
or else, a pressure cooker vent for joy.

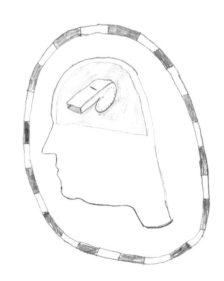

He bides his time, knowing each of us
will one day face encroaching dark, at last
may lick our lips and blow. He downs his pint
and whets his whistle, ready for the call.

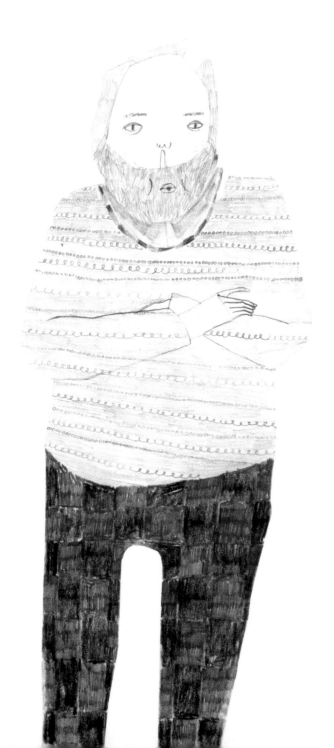

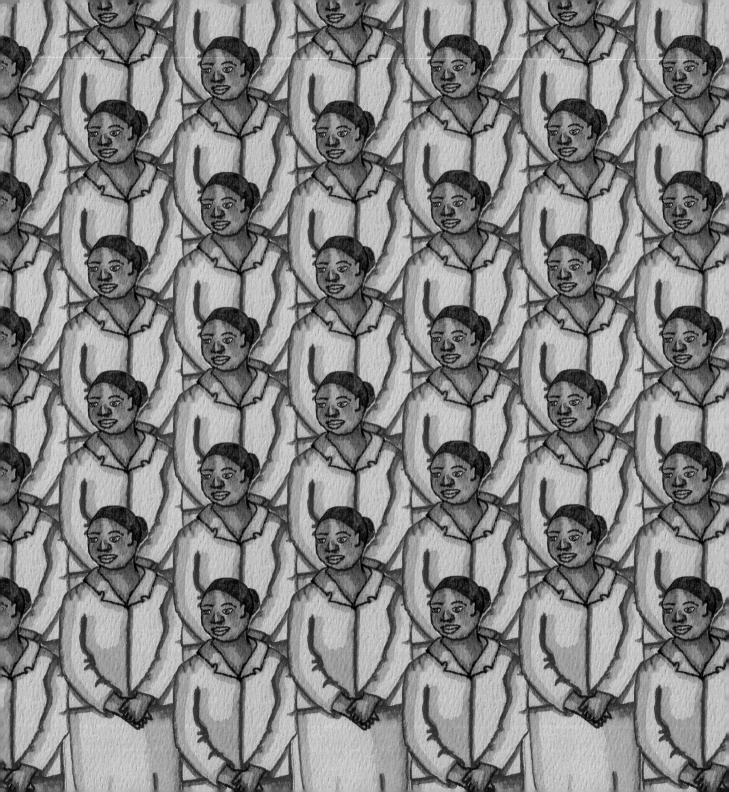

The Patron Saint of Conferences

An African-American woman in red uniform,
an earth-bound air hostess, is stationed
at the hub of the huge hotel, of a milling
mass of 9,000 delegates, calling out all day:
May I help someone?
May I help someone?

And they are drawn to her for guidance:
Down the hall. Up the elevator.
You're welcome. You're welcome.
All day her voice rises above the rabble.
A voice to lead a gospel choir, of a person
who has found her place in the world.

May I help someone?
May I help someone?
She casts the words about her
like a net of stars and stripes
gathering the shoals of poor,
the lost and huddled masses.

The Patron Saint of Ugly Towns

You've been to towns like this: shabby
as an old tramp, unwashed and moth-eaten,
shambling along from day to day; ringed
by black mountains, glowering against
the sun; paint peeling from the buildings
exposing plaster like old sores; a market
thronged with tired people in cheap shoes,
stalls heaped with out-size knickers, floral
aprons, itchy socks; a town where work
is history, mines closed, a slag heap
like their self-respect, where even stubby
trees refuse to grow, grass fails to root.
Out in fields the sunflowers bow their heavy
heads like congregations at a funeral,
listening to their doom, counting the hours.

My candles gutter in a grimy church
where mildew blooms on leaky walls,
and you might think my task as hopeless
as world peace. But watch me fly and brush
a feathered wing tip here or there:
a crow drops next year's sunflower seeds,
the gangly boy pulls down his cuffs and
slicks unruly hair for his first date,
a tabby cat twines round the widow's legs,
the too-young girl feels the first fluttering kicks.

Watch me fly, and see love shudder into life.

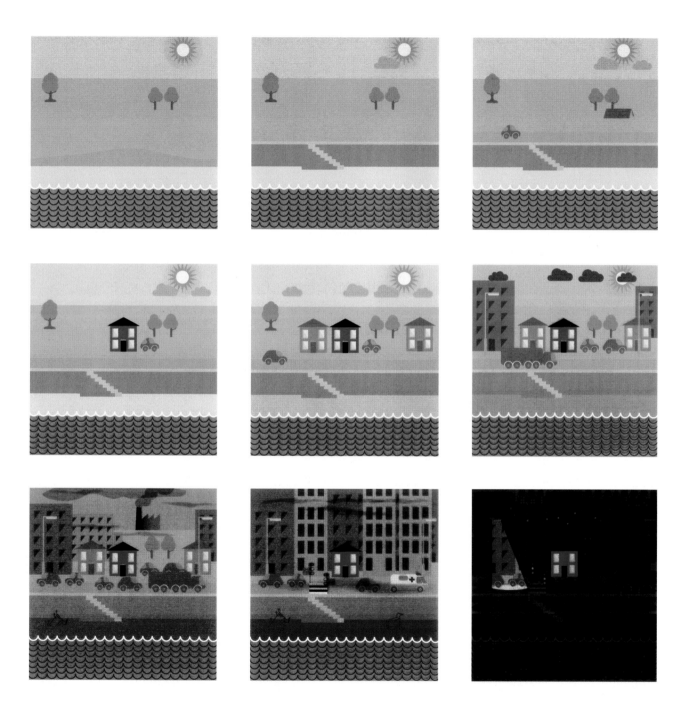

The (Official) Patron Saints of Poets

Brigid 453–523 AD0
Cecilia, died 117 AD
Columba 521–597 AD
David 1085–1015 BCE

Only these four are placed to catch our prayers
and bowl them onward to the heavenly stumps;

to be the friendly go-betweens who bide their time
dripping words of honey in the ear of God.

They have their other charges too, but none
they bend so fondly to as us, caress our hair.

Pray to them for reverie and peace, for threnody
and rhyme, for words which out-do death.

Illustration Credits

Front Cover	Kateryna Boiko
Final Page	Maj Abrahamsson
The Patron Saint of Remaindered Books	Birgit Linley
The Patron Saint of Careless Cyclists	Saki Watanabe
The Patron Saint of Missed Connections	Amy Johnson
The Patron Saint of Liars	Elizabeth Okori
The Patron Saint of Compulsive Hoarders	Amber Cooper Davies
The Patron Saint of Infidel Girls	Lefki Savvidou
The Patron Saint of the Un-Cool	Phil Shaw
The Patron Saint of Undelivered Letters	Zanna Allen
The Patron Saint of Naps	Fred Campbell
The Patron Saint of Rank Outsiders	Ben Hendy
The Patron Saint of Obsessive Housewives	Nancy Slonims
The Patron Saint of Sunday Morning	Abby Jones
The Patron Saint of Poetic Words	Samuel Gull
The Patron Saint of Weekends	Alex Foster
The Patron Saint of English Country Dancing	Fernanda Alonso
The Patron Saint of Sat Navs	Alexandra Vshivtseva
The Patron Saint of Tattoos	Hector Lloyd
The Patron Saint of Old Dogs	Fredrik Edén
The Patron Saint of Enthusiasts	Alex Moore
The Patron Saint of Eco-Warriors	Abigail Moulder
The Patron Saint of Bullies	Susan Light
The Patron Saint of Looters	Aldous Eveleigh
The Patron Saint of Soda Giants	Kremena Dimitrova
The Patron Saint of Hoods	Aleksandra Konoplina
The Patron Saint of Haunted Houses	Martin Ursell
The Patron Saint of Unwanted Hope	Darya Kurlyandtseva
The Patron Saint of The End of the World	Daniel Duncan
The Patron Saint of Whistling	Tony Allen
The Patron Saint of Conferences	Darja Kazijeva
The Patron Saint of Ugly Towns	Andrew Baker
The Patron Saint of Poets	Greta Mikalauskaite
End Papers	Paul Barritt

Other books by Maggie Butt

Poetry:
Quintana Roo; Acumen Publishing, 2003
Lipstick; Greenwich Exchange, 2007
I am the Sphinx (e-book and mp3); Snakeskin, 2009
petite; Hearing Eye, 2010
Ally Pally Prison Camp; Oversteps Books, 2011

Non-Fiction:
Story: The Heart of the Matter; Greenwich Exchange, 2007